THIS
NOTEBOOK
BELONGS TO..
THE
TAYLOR
SWIFT
EXPERIENCE
MW01631285

SHARE YOUR THOUGHTS AND DREAMS WITH TAYLOR SWIFT

SHARE YOUR THOUGHTS AND DREAMS WITH TAYLOR SWIFT

SHARE YOUR THOUGHTS AND DREAMS WITH TAYLOR SWIFT

SHARE YOUR THOUGHTS AND DREAMS WITH TAYLOR SWIFT

SHARE YOUR THOUGHTS AND DREAMS WITH TAYLOR SWIFT

SHARE YOUR THOUGHTS AND DREAMS WITH TAYLOR SWIFT

SHARE YOUR THOUGHTS AND DREAMS WITH TAYLOR SWIFT

SHARE YOUR THOUGHTS AND DREAMS WITH TAYLOR SWIFT

SHARE YOUR THOUGHTS AND DREAMS WITH TAYLOR SWIFT

SHARE YOUR THOUGHTS AND DREAMS WITH TAYLOR SWIFT

SHARE YOUR THOUGHTS AND DREAMS WITH TAYLOR SWIFT

SHARE YOUR THOUGHTS AND DREAMS WITH TAYLOR SWIFT

SHARE YOUR THOUGHTS AND DREAMS WITH TAYLOR SWIFT

SHARE YOUR THOUGHTS AND DREAMS WITH TAYLOR SWIFT

SHARE YOUR THOUGHTS AND DREAMS WITH TAYLOR SWIFT

SHARE YOUR THOUGHTS AND DREAMS WITH TAYLOR SWIFT

SHARE YOUR THOUGHTS AND DREAMS WITH TAYLOR SWIFT

SHARE YOUR THOUGHTS AND DREAMS WITH TAYLOR SWIFT

SHARE YOUR THOUGHTS AND DREAMS WITH TAYLOR SWIFT

SHARE YOUR THOUGHTS AND DREAMS WITH TAYLOR SWIFT

SHARE YOUR THOUGHTS AND DREAMS WITH TAYLOR SWIFT

SHARE YOUR THOUGHTS AND DREAMS WITH TAYLOR SWIFT

SHARE YOUR THOUGHTS AND DREAMS WITH TAYLOR SWIFT

SHARE YOUR THOUGHTS AND DREAMS WITH TAYLOR SWIFT

SHARE YOUR THOUGHTS AND DREAMS WITH TAYLOR SWIFT

SHARE YOUR THOUGHTS AND DREAMS WITH TAYLOR SWIFT

SHARE YOUR THOUGHTS AND DREAMS WITH TAYLOR SWIFT

SHARE YOUR THOUGHTS AND DREAMS WITH TAYLOR SWIFT

SHARE YOUR THOUGHTS AND DREAMS WITH TAYLOR SWIFT

SHARE YOUR THOUGHTS AND DREAMS WITH TAYLOR SWIFT

SHARE YOUR THOUGHTS AND DREAMS WITH TAYLOR SWIFT

SHARE YOUR THOUGHTS AND DREAMS WITH TAYLOR SWIFT

SHARE YOUR THOUGHTS AND DREAMS WITH TAYLOR SWIFT

SHARE YOUR THOUGHTS AND DREAMS WITH TAYLOR SWIFT

SHARE YOUR THOUGHTS AND DREAMS WITH TAYLOR SWIFT

SHARE YOUR THOUGHTS AND DREAMS WITH TAYLOR SWIFT

SHARE YOUR THOUGHTS AND DREAMS WITH TAYLOR SWIFT

SHARE YOUR THOUGHTS AND DREAMS WITH TAYLOR SWIFT

SHARE YOUR THOUGHTS AND DREAMS WITH TAYLOR SWIFT

SHARE YOUR THOUGHTS AND DREAMS WITH TAYLOR SWIFT

SHARE YOUR THOUGHTS AND DREAMS WITH TAYLOR SWIFT

SHARE YOUR THOUGHTS AND DREAMS WITH TAYLOR SWIFT

SHARE YOUR THOUGHTS AND DREAMS WITH TAYLOR SWIFT

SHARE YOUR THOUGHTS AND DREAMS WITH TAYLOR SWIFT

SHARE YOUR THOUGHTS AND DREAMS WITH TAYLOR SWIFT

SHARE YOUR THOUGHTS AND DREAMS WITH TAYLOR SWIFT

SHARE YOUR THOUGHTS AND DREAMS WITH TAYLOR SWIFT

SHARE YOUR THOUGHTS AND DREAMS WITH TAYLOR SWIFT

SHARE YOUR THOUGHTS AND DREAMS WITH TAYLOR SWIFT

SHARE YOUR THOUGHTS AND DREAMS WITH TAYLOR SWIFT

SHARE YOUR THOUGHTS AND DREAMS WITH TAYLOR SWIFT

SHARE YOUR THOUGHTS AND DREAMS WITH TAYLOR SWIFT

SHARE YOUR THOUGHTS AND DREAMS WITH TAYLOR SWIFT

SHARE YOUR THOUGHTS AND DREAMS WITH TAYLOR SWIFT

SHARE YOUR THOUGHTS AND DREAMS WITH TAYLOR SWIFT

SHARE YOUR THOUGHTS AND DREAMS WITH TAYLOR SWIFT

SHARE YOUR THOUGHTS AND DREAMS WITH TAYLOR SWIFT

SHARE YOUR THOUGHTS AND DREAMS WITH TAYLOR SWIFT

SHARE YOUR THOUGHTS AND DREAMS WITH TAYLOR SWIFT

SHARE YOUR THOUGHTS AND DREAMS WITH TAYLOR SWIFT

SHARE YOUR THOUGHTS AND DREAMS WITH TAYLOR SWIFT

SHARE YOUR THOUGHTS AND DREAMS WITH TAYLOR SWIFT

SHARE YOUR THOUGHTS AND DREAMS WITH TAYLOR SWIFT

SHARE YOUR THOUGHTS AND DREAMS WITH TAYLOR SWIFT

SHARE YOUR THOUGHTS AND DREAMS WITH TAYLOR SWIFT

SHARE YOUR THOUGHTS AND DREAMS WITH TAYLOR SWIFT

SHARE YOUR THOUGHTS AND DREAMS WITH TAYLOR SWIFT

SHARE YOUR THOUGHTS AND DREAMS WITH TAYLOR SWIFT

SHARE YOUR THOUGHTS AND DREAMS WITH TAYLOR SWIFT

SHARE YOUR THOUGHTS AND DREAMS WITH TAYLOR SWIFT

SHARE YOUR THOUGHTS AND DREAMS WITH TAYLOR SWIFT

SHARE YOUR THOUGHTS AND DREAMS WITH TAYLOR SWIFT

SHARE YOUR THOUGHTS AND DREAMS WITH TAYLOR SWIFT

SHARE YOUR THOUGHTS AND DREAMS WITH TAYLOR SWIFT

SHARE YOUR THOUGHTS AND DREAMS WITH TAYLOR SWIFT

SHARE YOUR THOUGHTS AND DREAMS WITH TAYLOR SWIFT

SHARE YOUR THOUGHTS AND DREAMS WITH TAYLOR SWIFT

SHARE YOUR THOUGHTS AND DREAMS WITH TAYLOR SWIFT

SHARE YOUR THOUGHTS AND DREAMS WITH TAYLOR SWIFT

SHARE YOUR THOUGHTS AND DREAMS WITH TAYLOR SWIFT

SHARE YOUR THOUGHTS AND DREAMS WITH TAYLOR SWIFT

SHARE YOUR THOUGHTS AND DREAMS WITH TAYLOR SWIFT

SHARE YOUR THOUGHTS AND DREAMS WITH TAYLOR SWIFT

SHARE YOUR THOUGHTS AND DREAMS WITH TAYLOR SWIFT

SHARE YOUR THOUGHTS AND DREAMS WITH TAYLOR SWIFT

SHARE YOUR THOUGHTS AND DREAMS WITH TAYLOR SWIFT

SHARE YOUR THOUGHTS AND DREAMS WITH TAYLOR SWIFT

SHARE YOUR THOUGHTS AND DREAMS WITH TAYLOR SWIFT

SHARE YOUR THOUGHTS AND DREAMS WITH TAYLOR SWIFT

SHARE YOUR THOUGHTS AND DREAMS WITH TAYLOR SWIFT

SHARE YOUR THOUGHTS AND DREAMS WITH TAYLOR SWIFT

SHARE YOUR THOUGHTS AND DREAMS WITH TAYLOR SWIFT

SHARE YOUR THOUGHTS AND DREAMS WITH TAYLOR SWIFT

SHARE YOUR THOUGHTS AND DREAMS WITH TAYLOR SWIFT

SHARE YOUR THOUGHTS AND DREAMS WITH TAYLOR SWIFT

SHARE YOUR THOUGHTS AND DREAMS WITH TAYLOR SWIFT

SHARE YOUR THOUGHTS AND DREAMS WITH TAYLOR SWIFT

SHARE YOUR THOUGHTS AND DREAMS WITH TAYLOR SWIFT

SHARE YOUR THOUGHTS AND DREAMS WITH TAYLOR SWIFT

SHARE YOUR THOUGHTS AND DREAMS WITH TAYLOR SWIFT

SHARE YOUR THOUGHTS AND DREAMS WITH TAYLOR SWIFT

SHARE YOUR THOUGHTS AND DREAMS WITH TAYLOR SWIFT

SHARE YOUR THOUGHTS AND DREAMS WITH TAYLOR SWIFT

SHARE YOUR THOUGHTS AND DREAMS WITH TAYLOR SWIFT

SHARE YOUR THOUGHTS AND DREAMS WITH TAYLOR SWIFT

SHARE YOUR THOUGHTS AND DREAMS WITH TAYLOR SWIFT

SHARE YOUR THOUGHTS AND DREAMS WITH TAYLOR SWIFT

SHARE YOUR THOUGHTS AND DREAMS WITH TAYLOR SWIFT

SHARE YOUR THOUGHTS AND DREAMS WITH TAYLOR SWIFT

Made in United States
Cleveland, OH
21 September 2025